NINE DAYS' WONDER

Performed in a dance from London to Norwich

WILLIAM KEMP

ISBN 978-1-905315-84-0 (paperback)

ISBN 978-1-905315-85-7 (ebook)

For more history books, news and features, visit

www.heritagehunter.co.uk

CONTENTS

INTRODUCTION

William Kempe, commonly known as Will Kemp, was a major name of his day as an actor, comedian and dancer, although few details of his life are certain.

It has been speculated that he was related to the wealthy Kempe family from near Ashford in Kent, but there is only circumstantial evidence for this. He is first mentioned for certain as a performer with the Earl of Leicester's Players in the 1580s, and it is suggested he may have therefore been born around 1560. He performed with these players in the Netherlands in 1585–6, and was even employed by Sir Philip Sidney to carry letters home… which he delivered to the wrong lady, which caused some embarrassment.

Kemp was soon known for his physical comedy in particular, becoming a natural successor to the famous clown Richard Tarlton, who died in 1588: in 1590 Kemp was described by playwright Thomas Nashe as "that most comical and conceited cavalier, Monsieur du Kemp, jestmonger and vice-gerent general to the ghost of Dick Tarlton". In 1599, Ben Jonson alluded to Kemp throwing his shoe at another player. Kemp was also renowned for his jigs – comic skits and song and dance routines which perhaps bring to mind the music halls of the Victorian era.

In 1592–4, Kemp was performing with Lord Strange's Men, and performed at the Rose in Southwark, before joining the Lord Chamberlain's Men in company with celebrated actor Richard Burbage and one William Shakespeare. Kemp performed in several of Shakespeare's early comedies, and is even believed to have created the character of Falstaff.

Around 1599, though, he seems to have fallen out with the Lord Chamberlain's Men and pursued what we might call a solo career. (Why is unclear – possibly he was superseded, although he had shares in the Globe Theatre, or his style of comedy fell out of favour.)

The first and well-known direction this took him in was his 110-mile morris dance from London to Norwich in February–March 1600, which he recounted in *Kemp's Nine Daies Wonder*, the present volume.

As can be seen, he quickly fell victim to the inaccuracies of the press of his day – the ballad writers – and he goes to great lengths here (especially in the afterword) to taken them to task for it. He also suggests he had another picaresque adventure in mind, though we don't know if he carried it out.

There is circumstantial evidence that in 1601 he travelled in Europe, to Germany and Italy, and possibly led a company of performers in the Netherlands. In 1602 he was back in England with Worcester's Men and then the trail goes cold again. On 2 November 1603, 'Kemp, a man' was buried in Southwark; although a William Kempe is mentioned as a servant to Lady Hunsdon in 1610, and there are other allusions to him around then, although share documents for the Globe Theatre make it certain he was dead by 1615. We do have poet Richard Braithwait's 1618 epitaph to Kemp:

> Welcome from Norwich, Kempe! all joy to see
> Thy safe return moriscoed lustily.
> But out, alas, how soon's thy morice done!
> When Pipe and Taber, all thy friends be gone,
> And leave thee now to dance the second part
> With feeble nature, not with nimble Art;
> Then all thy triumphs fraught with strains of mirth
> Shall be cag'd up within a chest of earth:
> Shall be? they are: th'ast danc'd thee out of breath,
> And now must make thy parting dance with death.

Ultimately, Kemp's name lives on for his association with Shakespeare, and for this eccentric dancing journey to Norwich. He could be seen, perhaps, as the comedic forefather of modern adventurers travelling around Ireland with a fridge or undertaking a psychogeographical circumambulation of the M25. His account is knowing and entertaining, as well as appreciative of the kindness of strangers as he capered his way across East Anglia. Daryl W. Palmer describes "Kemp's brilliant but neglected prose as one of the earliest and brightest re-presentations of what we would today call 'performance art'".[1]

Kemp has appeared as a character in many stories since, from the Elizabethan *Parnassus* plays contemporary with his "wild morrise to Norrige" (in playwright William Rowley's words from 1609) to *Doctor Who* and *The Upstart Crow* today. His morris dance was reenacted by comedian Tim FitzHigham in 2008 and has inspired numerous plays and retellings. The dance goes on.

Andrew Chapman

A note on the text: the main edition of *Kemp's Nine Daies Wonder* was edited by the Rev Alexander Dyce in 1840 (he transcribed the only surviving original copy of Kemp's pamphlet, held in the Bodleian Library, Oxford) and is freely available at Project Gutenberg and the Internet Archive. I have used Professor Edward Arber's 1909 version from *An English Garner*, which modernised Kemps' Elizabethan spellings. Annotations here (in square brackets or endnotes) are derived from both Dyce and Arber, with my own additions.

---

1. 'William Kemp's Nine Daies Wonder and the Transmission of Performance Culture', *Journal of Dramatic Theory and Criticism* 1991 5(2).

Kemp's nine days' wonder.

Performed in a dance from London to Norwich.
Containing the Pleasure, Pains, and kind Entertainment of WILLIAM KEMP, between London and that city, in his late Morrice.
Wherein is somewhat set down worth note, to reprove the slanders spread of him; many things merry, nothing hurtful.
Written by himself, to satisfy his friends.

LONDON:
Printed by E. A. for NICHOLAS LING, and are to be sold at his shop, at the West Door of Saint Paul's Church.
1600

To the true ennobled Lady, and his most bountiful Mistress, Mistress ANNE FITTON,[1] Maid of Honour to the most sacred Maid Royal, QUEEN ELIZABETH.

Honourable Mistress.

In the wane of my little wit, I am forced to desire your protection; else every ballad singer will proclaim me bankrupt of honesty! A sort of mad fellows, seeing me merrily disposed in a Morrice, have so bepainted me in print, since my gambols began from London to Norwich, that (having but an ill face before) I shalt appear to the world without a face, if your fair hand wipe not away their foul colours.

One hath written *Kemp's farewell*, to the tune of *Kery, mery, buffe*; another, his *desperate dangers in his late travail*; the third, his *entertainment to Newmarket*, which town I came never near, by the length of half the heath. Some swear in a *trenchmore* [*a lively dance*], I have trod a good way to win the world; others that guess righter, affirm, "I have without good help, danced myself out of the world!" Many say many things that were never thought.

But, in a word, your poor Servant offers the truth of his Progress and profit, to your honourable view! receive it, I beseech you! such as it is, rude and plain: for I know your pure judgement looks as soon to see beauty in a blackamoor, or hear smooth speech from a stammerer, as to find anything but blunt mirth in a Morrice dancer! especially such a one as WILL KEMP, that hath spent his life in mad jigs and merry jests.

Three reasons move me to make public this journey. One, to reprove lying fools I never knew. The other, to commend loving friends, which, by the way, I daily found. The third, to show my duty to your honourable self. Whose favours, among other bountiful friends, make me, despite of this sad world, judge my heart Cork, and my heels Feathers: so that, methinks, I could fly to Rome (at least, hop to Rome, as the old proverb is) with a mortar on my head.

In which light conceit, I lowly beg pardon and leave: for my tabourer strikes his *Hunt's up*! I must to Norwich!

Imagine, noble Mistress! I am now setting from my Lord Mayor's! the hour, about seven! the morning, gloomy! the company, many! my heart, merry!

Your worthy Ladyship's
Most unworthy servant,
WILLIAM KEMP.

1. Anne Fitton (later Anne Newdigate) was a gentlewoman, daughter of Sir Edward Fitton, known for the British plantation of Ireland – but Anne was not a maid of honour to Elizabeth I… Her sister Mary was, however, so Kemp may have muddled them. Mary had a variety of scandalous affairs and has been suggested as the 'Dark Lady' of Shakespeare's sonnets.

THE FIRST DAY'S JOURNEY

BEING THE FIRST MONDAY IN CLEAN LENT; FROM THE RIGHT HONOURABLE THE LORD MAYOR'S, OF LONDON

KEMP's nine days' wonder.
Performed 1n a Morrice from London to Norwich.
Wherein every day's journey is pleasantly set down, to satisfy his friends [as to] the truth; against all lying ballad-makers: what he did, how he was welcome, and by whom entertained.

The first Monday in Lent [Feb. II, 1600], the close morning promising a clear day; attended on by Thomas Slye, my Tabourer; William Bee, my servant; and George Sprat appointed for my Overseer, that I should take no other ease, but my prescribed order: myself, that's I (otherwise called *Cavaliero* KEMP, Head Master of Morrice dancers, High Headborough of heighs, and only tricker of your Trill-lilles, and best bell-shangles [*fool*], between Sion and Mount Surrey)[1] began frolicly to foot it, from the Right Honourable the Lord Mayor's, of London, towards the Right Worshipful and truly bountiful Master Mayor's at Norwich.

My setting forward was somewhat before seven in the morning, my Tabourer struck up merrily, and as fast as kind people thronging together would give me leave, through London, I leapt!

By the way, many good old people, and divers others of younger years, of mere kindness, give me bowed [*bent*] sixpences and groats; blessing me with their hearty prayers and "God speeds!"

Being past Whitechapel, and having left fair London,with all that north-east suburb before named, multitudes of Londoners left not me! but either to keep a custom that many hold, that "Mile End is no walk, without a recreation at Stratford [at] Bow, with cream and cakes," or else for love they bear towards me, or perhaps to make themselves merry if I should chance, as many thought, to give over my Morrice within a mile of Mile End.

However, many a thousand brought me to Bow; where I rested a while from dancing: but had small rest with those, that would have urged me to drinking. But, I warrant you! WILL. KEMP was wise enough! To their full cups, "kind thanks!" was my return; with gentlemanlike protestations, as "Truly, Sir, I dare not! It stands not with the congruity of my health!"

"Congruity," said I! but how came that strange language in my mouth? I think scarcely that it is any Christian word: and yet it may be a good word, for ought I know; though I never made it, nor do very well understand it! Yet I am sure, I have bought it at the wordmongers, at as dear a rate as I could have had a whole hundred of bavins [*logs*] from the woodmongers.

Farewell "Congruity!" for I mean now to be more concise, and stand upon evener bases! but I must neither stand nor sit, the Tabourer strikes alarum. "Tickle it, good

Tom! I'll follow thee! Farewell Bow! Have over the Bridge, where, I heard say, 'Honest Conscience was once drowned.' It is pity if it were so! but that is no matter belonging to our Morrice; let us now along to Stratford Langton!"

Many good fellows being there met, and knowing how well I loved the sport, had prepared a Bear baiting: but so unreasonable were the multitudes of people, that I could only hear the bear roar and the dogs howl. Therefore forward I went, with my hey de gaies [*a rural dance*] to Ilford, where I again rested; and was by the people of the town and country thereabouts, very well welcomed: being offered carouses in the great spoon, one whole draught [of it] being able at that time to have drawn my little wit dry; but being afraid of the old proverb, *He had need of a long spoon that eats with the Devil*, I soberly gave my boon companions the slip.

From Ilford, by moonshine, I set forward, dancing within a quarter of a mile of Romford: where in the highway, two strong jades, having belike some quarrel to me unknown, were beating and biting of each other; and such, through God's help, was my good hap that I escaped their hoofs, both being raised with their forefeet above my head, like two smiths over one anvil.

There, being an end of my First Day's Morrice, a kind gentleman of London [a]lighting from his horse, would have no "Nay!" but I should leap into his saddle. To be plain with ye! I was not proud; but took kindly his kindlier offer, chiefly thereto urged by my weariness. So I rode to my inn at Romford.

In that town, to give rest to my well laboured limbs, I continued two days: being much beholden to the towns men for their love; but more to the Londoners, that came hourly thither in great numbers, to visit me, offering much more kindness than I was willing to accept.

---

1. Mount Syon is a country house near Brentford; Mount Surrey was a mansion near Norwich.

THE SECOND DAY'S JOURNEY

BEING THURSDAY OF THE FIRST WEEK

Thursday [*Feb.* 14, 1600], being market day at Burnt Wood, Tom Slye was earlier up than the lark, and sounded merrily the Morrice. I roused myself, and returned from Romford to the place where I took horse the first night; dancing that quarter of a mile back again, through Romford, and so merrily to Burnt Wood.

Yet now I remember it well, I had no great cause of mirth! For at Romford town's end, I strained my hip; and, for a time, endured exceeding pain: but being loth to trouble a surgeon, I held on, finding remedy by labour that had hurt me. For it came in a turn; and so, in my dance, I turned it out of my service again.

The multitudes were so great, at my coming to Burnt Wood, that I had much ado (though I made many entreaties and stays) to get passage to my inn.

In this town, two cut-purses [*pickpockets*] were taken, that with other two of their companions followed me from London; as many better disposed people did. But these two dy-doppers gave out, when they were apprehended, that "they had laid wagers, and betted about my journey."

Whereupon the Officers bringing them to my inn, I justly denied their acquaintance; saving that "I remembered one of them to be a noted cut-purse:" such a one as we tie to a post on our Stage, for all people to wonder at; when at a Play, they are taken pilfering.

This fellow and his half-brother being found with the deed, were sent to gaol: their other two consorts had the charity of the town! and, after a dance of *Trenchmore* at the whipping cross, they were sent back to London; where, I am afraid, there are too many of their occupation. To be short, I thought myself well rid of four such followers; and I wish heartily, that the whole world were clear of such companions!

Having rested well at Burnt Wood, the moon shining clearly and the weather being calm, in the evening, I tripped it to Ingerstone; stealing away from those numbers of people that followed me: yet, do what I could, I had above fifty in the company, some of London, the others of the country thereabouts; that would needs, when they heard my taber, trudge after me through thick and thin.

THE THIRD DAY'S JOURNEY

BEING FRIDAY OF THE FIRST WEEK

On Friday morning [*Feb.* 15, 1600], I set forward towards Chelmsford, not having past two hundred; being the least company that I had in the day time between London and that place.

Onward I went, thus easily followed, till I came to Witford Bridge: where a number of country gentlemen and gentlewomen were gathered together to see me. Sir Thomas Mildmay[1] standing at his park pale [*palings*], received gently a pair of garters of me: gloves, points, and garters being my ordinary merchandise, that I put to venture for performance of my merry voyage.

So much ado I had to pass by the people at Chelmsford, that it was more than an hour ere I could recover my inn gate; where I was fain to lock myself in my chamber, and pacify them with words out of a window instead of deeds. To deal plainly, I was so weary that I could dance no more.

The next morning, I footed it three miles of my way towards Braintree: but returned back again to Chelmsford; where I lay that Saturday and the next Sunday.

The good cheer and kind welcome I had at Chelmsford

was much more than I was willing to entertain: for my only desire was to refrain from drink, and be temperate in my diet.

At Chelmsford, a maid not passing fourteen years of age, dwelling with one Sudley my kind friend, made request to her Master and Dame, that she might dance the Morrice with me, in a great large room. They being intreated, I was soon won to fit her with bells; besides [which], she would have the old fashion, with napkin on [each of] her arms: and to our jumps, we fell!

A whole hour, she held out! but then, being ready to lie down, I left her off: but thus much in her praise, I would have challenged the strongest man in Chelmsford; and amongst many, I think few would have done so much.

---

1. Sir Thomas Mildmay was a courtier and local official.

THE FOURTH DAY'S JOURNEY

BEING MONDAY OF THE SECOND WEEK

On Monday morning [*Feb.* 18], very early, I rode the three miles I danced the Saturday before; where, alighting, my Tabourer struck up, and lightly I tripped forward: but I had the heaviest way that ever mad Morrice dancer trod: yet

With hey and ho! through thick and thin;
The hobby horse quite forgotten
I followed as I did begin!
Although the way were rotten.

This foul way I could find no ease in, thick woods being on either side the lane; the lane likewise being full of deep holes, sometimes I skipped up to the waist! But it is an old proverb, that *it is a little comfort to the miserable, to have companions*: and amidst this miry way, I had some mirth, by an unlooked for accident.

It was the custom of honest country fellows, my unknown friends, upon hearing of my pipe (which might well be heard, in a still morning or evening, a mile), to get up and bear me company a little way.

In this foul way, two pretty plain youths watched me; and with their kindness somewhat hindered me. One, a fine light fellow, would be still before me; the other, ever at my heels!

At length, coming to a broad plash of water and mud, which could not be avoided; I fetched a rise, yet fell in over the ankles at the further end. My youth that followed me, took his jump, and stuck fast in the midst, crying out to his companion, "Come, George! call ye this dancing! I'll go no further!" for, indeed, he could go no further, till his fellow was fain to wade and help him out. I could not choose but laugh, to see how, like two frogs, they laboured!

A hearty farewell, I gave them! And they faintly bade "God speed me!" saying if I danced that dirty way, this seven years' again, they would never dance after me!

Well, with much ado, I got unto Braintree, by noon, and tarried there Monday night and the next day; only I danced three miles on Tuesday, to ease my Wednesday's journey.

If I should deny that I was welcome at Braintree, I should slander an honest crew of kind men; among whom, I fared well, slept well, and was every way well used.

THE FIFTH DAY'S JOURNEY

BEING WEDNESDAY OF THE SECOND WEEK

Taking advantage of my three miles that I had danced the day before; this Wednesday morning [*Feb.* 20], I tripped it to Sudbury; whither came to see me, a very kind Gentleman, Master Foskew, that had, before, travelled afoot from London to Berwick: who, giving me good counsel to observe temperate diet for my health, and other advice to be careful of my company, besides his liberal entertainment, departed; leaving me much indebted to his love.

In this town of Sudbury, there came a lusty tall fellow, a butcher by his profession, that would, in a Morrice, keep me company to Bury. I being glad of his friendly offer, gave him thanks: and forward we did set! But ere ever we had measured half a mile of our way, he gave me over in the plain field: protesting that "if he might get a hundred pounds, he would not hold out with me!" For, indeed, my pace in dancing is not ordinary.

As he and I were parting, a lusty country lass being among the people, called him "Faint-hearted lout!" saying,

"If I had begun to dance, I would have held out one mile, though it had cost my life!"

At which words, many laughed.

"Nay," saith she, "if the Dancer will lend me a leash of his bells, I'll venture to tread one mile with him, myself!"

I looked upon her, saw mirth in her eyes, heard boldness in her words, and beheld her ready to tuck up her russet petticoat. I fitted her with bells, which she, merrily taking, garnished her thick short legs: and with a smooth brow, bade the Tabourer begin.

The drum struck, forward march I, with my merry Maid Marian: who shook her fat sides, and footed it merrily to Melford; being a long mile.

There parting with her, I gave her, besides her skin full of drink, an English crown to buy more drink: for, good wench! she was in a piteous heat!

My kindness she requited with dropping some dozen of short courtsies [*curtsies*], and bidding "God bless the Dancer!"

I bad her "Adieu!" and to give her her due, she had a good ear, danced truly: and we parted friendly.

But ere I part with her, a good fellow, my friend, having writ an odd rhyme of her, I will set it down.

A country lass (brown as a berry,
Blithe of blee, in heart as merry;
Cheeks well fed, and sides well larded;
Every bone, with fat flesh guarded)
Meeting merry Kemp by chance,
Was Marian in his Morrice dance.
Her stump legs, with bells were garnished:
Her brown brows, with sweating varnished;
Her brown hips, when she was lag,
To win her ground, went swig-a-swag:

Which to see, all that came after
Were replete with mirthful laughter.
Yet she thumped it on her way
With a sportly *hey de gay*!
At a mile, her dance she ended;
Kindly paid, and well commended.

At Melford, diverse Gentlemen met me, who brought me to one Master Colts, a very kind and worshipful Gentleman: where I had unexpected entertainment till the Saturday.

From whose house, having hope somewhat to amend my way to Bury, I determined to go by Clare: but I found it both further and fouler.

THE SIXTH DAY'S JOURNEY

BEING SATURDAY OF THE SECOND WEEK

From Wednesday night till Saturday, having been troublesome, but much more welcome to Master Colts; in the morning [*Feb.* 23], I took my leave, and was accompanied with many Gentlemen, a mile of my way. Which mile, Master Colts's Fool would needs dance with me, and had his desire; where leaving me, two fools parted fair in a foul way: I keeping on my course to Clare, where I a while rested; and then cheerfully set forward to Bury [St. Edmunds].

Passing from Clare, towards Bury, I was invited to the house of a very bountiful widow, whose husband, during his life, was a yeoman of that country, dying rich, no doubt! as might well appear by the riches and plenty that abounded in every corner of the house. She is called the Widow Everet.

At her house were met above thirty Gentlemen. Such, and so plentiful variety of good fare, I have very seldom seen in any Commoner's house. Her behaviour being very modest and friendly, argued her bringing up not to be rude. She was a woman of good presence; and, if a Fool may judge! of no small discretion.

From this widow's, I danced to Bury; coming in on the Saturday, in the afternoon: at what time, the Right Honourable the Lord Chief Justice[1] entered at another gate of the town. The wondering and regardless multitude making his Honour clear way, left the streets where he passed, to gape at me: the throng of them being so great, that poor WILL. KEMP was seven times stayed, ere he could recover his inn.

By reason of the great snow that then fell, I stayed at Bury from Saturday in the Second week of my setting forth, till Thursday night, the next week following.

---

1. This is Sir John Popham (1531–1607), who held the role from 1592 to 1607 and was noted for his severity.

THE SEVENTH DAY'S JOURNEY

BEING FRIDAY OF THE THIRD WEEK

Upon Friday morning [*Feb.* 29] I set on towards Thetford, dancing that ten miles in three hours: for I left Bury somewhat after seven in the morning, and was at Thetford somewhat after ten that same forenoon.

But, indeed, considering how I had been booted [*his buskins covered with mud*] before, and that all this way, or the most of it, was over a heath; it was no great wonder. For I fared like one that had escaped the stocks, and tried the use of his legs to outrun the Constable; so light were my heels, that I counted the ten miles no better than a leap.

At my entrance into Thetford, the people came in great numbers to see me: for there were many there, it being Assize time.

The noble Gentleman, Sir Edwin Rich,[1] gave me entertainment in such bountiful and liberal sort during my continuance there Saturday and Sunday, that I want fit words to express the least part of his worthy usage of my unworthiness: and to conclude liberally, as he had begun and continued; at my departure on Monday, his Worship gave me five pounds.

---

1. Rich was knighted at Cádiz in 1596 in the expedition to capture the city from Spain.

THE EIGHTH DAY'S JOURNEY

BEING MONDAY OF THE FOURTH WEEK

On Monday morning [*March* 3] I danced to Rockland ere I rested; and coming to my inn, where the host was a very boon companion, I desired to see him: but in no case, he would be spoken with, till he had shifted himself from his working days' suit.

Being armed at all points, from the cap to the foot, his black shoes shining and made straight with copper buckles of the best, his garters in the fashion, and every garment fitting *corremsquandam*, to use his own word; he enters the hall, with his bonnet in his hand, and began to cry out, "0 KEMP! dear Master KEMP! You are even as welcome as, as, as," and so stammering he began to study for a fit comparison (and I thank him, at last he fitted me!) for, saith he, "thou art even as welcome as the Queen's best greyhound!"

After this dogged yet well-meaning salutation, the carouses were called in; and my friendly host of Rockland began with, "All this!" blessing the hour upon his knees, that "any of the Queen's Majesty's well-willers or friends would vouchsafe to come within his house!" as if never any such had been within his doors before.

I took his good meaning, and gave him great thanks for his kindness.

And having rested me well, I began to take my course for Hingham, whither my honest host of Rockland would needs be my guide: but, good true fat-belly! he had not followed me two fields, but he lay along and cried after me, to come back and speak with him.

I fulfilled his request, and coming to him, "Dancer!" quoth he, "if thou dance, in God's name! God speed thee! I cannot follow thee a foot further! but adieu, good Dancer! God speed thee, if thou dance in God's name!"

I having haste of my way, and he being able to keep no way, we parted. Farewell, he! He was a kind good fellow, a true Troyan! and [if] it ever be my luck to meet him at more leisure, I'll make him full amends with a cupful of Canary.

But now I am a little better advised, we must not thus let my mad host pass! For my friend, late mentioned before, that made the odd rhyme on my Maid Marian, would needs remember my Host! Such as it is, I'll bluntly set down!

He was a man not over spare,
In his eyeballs dwelt no care:
"Anon, anon!" and "Welcome, friend!"
Were the most words he used to spend.
Save, sometimes, he would sit and tell
What wonders once in Boulogne fell![1]
Closing each period of his tale,
With a full cup of nutbrown ale.
Tourwin and Tournay's sieges were hot,[2]
Yet all my host remembers not.
Kett's Field[3] and Musselborough[4] fray
Were battles fought but yesterday.

"O 'twas a goodly matter then
To see your sword and buckler men!
There would lie here! and here! and there!
But I would meet them everywhere.
And now a man is but a prick.
A boy armed with a poating stick[5]
Will dare to challenge Cutting Dick.[6]
O 'tis a world! the world to see;
But 'twill not mend for thee or me!"
By this, some guest cries, "Ho! the house!"
A fresh friend hath a fresh carouse!
Still he will drink, and still be dry:
And quaff with every company.
Saint Martin send him merry mates
To enter at his hostree [*hostelry*] gates!
For a blither lad than he
Cannot an Innkeeper be.

Well, once again, farewell, my host at Rockland!

After all these farewells, I am sure, to Hingham I found a foul way; as before I had done from Thetford to Rockland.

Yet, besides the deep way, I was much hindered by the desire people had to see me.

For even as our shopkeepers will haul, and pull a man, with, "Lack ye! What do you lack, Gentlemen?" "My ware is best!" cries one. "Mine [the] best in England!" says another. "Here, you shall have choice!" saith the third: so were the diverse voices of the young men and maidens which I should meet at every mile's end; thronging by twenty, and sometimes forty, yea, hundreds in a company. One cried "the fairest way was through their village!" another, "This is the nearest and fairest way, when you have passed but a mile and a half!" another sort cry, "Turn on the left hand!" some "on the right hand!" that I was so amazed, I knew not sometimes which way I might best take but haphazard, the people still accompanying me, whereat I was much comforted, though the ways were bad. But, as I said before, at last I overtook it.

---

1. This refers to the 1544 siege of Boulogne, when Henry VIII took the town.
2. Both towns that surrendered to Henry VII too.
3. A battle in 1549 near Norwich, when Robert Kett and other rebels stormed Norwich in response to land enclosure.
4. The battle of Pinkie Cleugh in 1547, the last pitched battle (i.e. at an agreed location) between Scotland and England.
5. A poating stick was used for setting the plaits of a ruff collar.
6. A character from a play.

THE NINTH DAY'S JOURNEY

BEING WEDNESDAY OF THE FOURTH WEEK

The next morning [*March* 5] I left Hingham, not staying till I came to Barford Bridge, five young men running all the way with me; for otherwise my pace was not for footmen.

From Barford Bridge, I danced to Norwich [*eight miles*]. But coming within sight of the city, perceiving so great a multitude and throng of people still crowding more and more about me: mistrusting it would be a let [*hindrance*] to my determined expedition and pleasurable humour, which I, long before, conceived, to delight this city with (so far as my best skill and industry of my long travelled sinews could afford them): I was advised, and so took ease by that advice, to stay my Morrice a little above St. Giles's Gate; where I took my gelding, and so rode into the city, procrastinating my merry Morrice dance through the city till better opportunity.

Being come within the city, Master Roger Weild the Mayor, and sundry others of his worshipful Brethren, sent for me. Who perceiving how I intended not to dance into the city that night, and being well satisfied with the reasons;

they allotted me time enough not to dance until Saturday after: to the end, that diverse Knights and Gentlemen, together with their wives and children, who had been many days before deceived with expectation of my coming, might now, have sufficient warning accordingly, by Saturday following.

In the mean space, and during my still continuance in the city afterwards, they not only very courteously offered to bear mine own charges and my followers; but very bountifully performed it at the common charges. The Mayor and many of the Aldermen, oftentimes besides, invited us privately to their several houses.

To make a short end of this tedious description of my entertainment.

Saturday [*March* 8] no sooner came, but I returned without the city, through St. Giles's Gate; and began my Morrice where I left, at that Gate. But I entered in at St. Stephen's Gate,where one Thomas Gilbert, in the name of all the rest of the city, gave me a friendly and exceeding kind welcome: which I have no reason to omit, unless I would condemn myself of ingratitude; partly for the private affection of the writer towards me, as also for the general love and favour I found in them, from the highest to the lowest, the richest as the poorest.

It follows in these few lines.

Master KEMP his welcome to Norwich.

W With heart and hand, among the rest,
E Especially you welcome are!
L Long looked for, as welcome guest:
C Come, now at last! you be from far.
O Of most within the city, sure,
M Many good wishes you have had!

E Each one did pray, you might endure

W With courage good, the match you made!
I Intend they did, with gladsome hearts,
L Like your well-willers, you to meet!

K Know you also, they'll do their parts,
E Either in field or house, to greet
M More you, than any with you came,
P Procured thereto, with trump and fame.

Your well-willer,
T. G.

Passing the gate, there were Whifflers, such Officers as were appointed by the Mayor, to make me way through the throng of the people which pressed so mightily upon me. With great labour, I got through that narrow press, into the open Market Place.

Where, on the Cross, ready prepared, stood the City Waits, which not a little refreshed my weariness,with toiling through so narrow a lane as the people left me. Such Waits (under *Benedicite* be it spoken) few cities in our realm have the like, none better! Who, besides their excellency in wind instruments, and their rare cunning on the viol and violin: their voices are admirable! every one of them able to serve in any Cathedral church in Christendom for choristers.

Passing by the Market Place, the press still increasing by the number of boys, girls, men, and women, thronging more and more before me, to see the end; it was the mischance of a homely maid (that, belike, was but newly crept into the fashion of long-waisted petticoats tied with points [*laces or tags*]; and had, as it seemed, but one point tied before) that coming unluckily in my way, as I was fetching a leap, it fell out, that I set my foot on her skirts. The point either breaking or stretching, off fell her petticoat from her waist! but, as chance was, though her smock was coarse, it was cleanly.

Yet the poor wench was so ashamed, the rather for that she could hardly recover her [petti]coat again from unruly boys; that looking before like one that had the green sickness, now had she her cheeks all coloured with scarlet.

I was sorry for her, but on I went towards the Mayor's: and deceived the people, by leaping over the Churchyard wall at St. John's; getting so into Master Mayor's gates a nearer way.

But, at last, I found it the further way about: being forced, on the Tuesday following [*March* ww], to renew my former dance; because George Sprat, my Overseer, having lost me in the throng, would not be deposed that I had danced it, since he saw me not. And I must confess, I did not well: for the citizens had caused all the turnpikes to be taken up on Saturday, that I might not be hindered.

But now I return again to my jump, the measure of which is to be seen in the Guildhall at Norwich; where my buskins, that I then wore and danced in from London thither, stand, equally divided, nailed on the wall.

The plenty of good cheer at the Mayor's, his bounty and kind usage; together with the general welcomes of his worshipful Brethren and many others, Knights, Ladies, Gentlemen, and Gentlewomen, so much exceeded my expectation, as I adjudged myself most bound to them all.

The Mayor gave me five pounds in Elizabeth Angels [*gold coins*]; which Mayor, (*fair Madame! to whom I too presumptuously dedicate my idle paces!*) as a man worthy of singular and impartial admiration, if our critic humourous minds could as prodigally conceive as he desires, for his chaste life, liberality, and temperance in possessing worldly benefits. He lives unmarried and childless: and never purchased house nor land; the house he dwells in, this year, being but hired. He lives upon merchandise; being a Merchant Venturer.

If our Merchants and Gentlemen would take example by this man, Gentlemen would not sell their lands, to become bankrupt Merchants; nor Merchants live in the possessions of youth-beguiled Gentlemen; who cast themselves out of their parents' heritages for a few outcast commodities. But Wit! whither wilt thou? What hath Morrice-tripping WILL. to do with that? It keeps not time with his dance! Therefore, room you! moral precepts! Give my legs leave to end my Morrice! or that being ended, my hands leave to perfect this worthless poor tottered [*? tattered*] volume!

Pardon me, Madam! that I am thus tedious! I cannot choose but commend sacred liberality, which makes poor wretches partakers of all comfortable benefits!

Besides the love and favour already repeated, Master Weild, the Mayor, gave me 40s. yearly, during my life, making me a Freeman of the Merchant Venturers.

This is the substance of all my journey. Therefore let no man believe (however before, by lying Ballets and rumours they have been abused) that either ways were laid open for me, or that I delivered gifts to Her Majesty.

It is good being merry, my Masters! but in a mean! and all my mirths, mean though they be, have been and ever shall be employed to the delight of my royal Mistress! whose sacred Name ought not to be remembered among such ribald rhymes as these late thin-breeched lying Ballet singers have proclaimed it.

. . .

It resteth now, that, in a word, I shew what profit I have made by my Morrice.

True it is, I put out some money to have threefold gain at my return [*i.e. he accepted bets of three to one that he could not dance this Morris to Norwich*]. Some that love me, regard my pains and respect their promise, [and] have sent home the treble worth. Some others, at the first sight, have paid me, if I came to seek them. Others I cannot see, nor will they be willingly found! and these are the greater number.

If they had all used me well; or all, ill: I would have boldly set down the true sum of my small gain or loss! but I will have patience some few days longer.

At the end of which time, if any be behind, I will draw a Catalogue of all their names I ventured with. Those that have shewn themselves honest men; I will set before them this character, **H.** for Honesty. Before the other bench whistlers shall stand **K.** for Ketlers or Keistrels, that will drive a good companion, without need in them, to contend for his own. But I hope I shall have no such need!

If I have, your honourable protection shall thus far defend your poor servant, that he may, being a plain man, call a spade a spade.

Thus, fearing your Ladyship is wearier with reading this toy than I was in all my merry travail; I crave pardon! and conclude this first pamphlet that ever WILL. KEMP offered to the Press: being thereunto pressed on the one side by the pitiful papers pasted on every post, of that which was neither so, nor so; and, on the other side, urged thereto in duty, to express with thankfulness the kind entertainment I found.

Your Honour's poor servant,

W. K.

AFTERWORD

KEMP's humble request to the impudent generation of Ballad-makers and their coherents, that it would please their Rascalities to pity his pains in the great journey he pretends [intends]; and not fill the country with lies of his never-done acts, as they did in his late Morrice to Norwich.

To the tune of Thomas Deloney's Epitaph.[1]

My notable Shake-rags!

The effect of my suit is discovered in the title of my Supplication.

But for your better understandings, for that I know you to be a sort of witless beetle-heads that can understand nothing but what is knocked into your scalps, These are, by these presents, to certify unto your Blockheadships, that I, William Kemp, whom you had near hand-rent in sunder, with your unreasonable rhymes, and shortly, God willing! to set forward (as merrily as I may), whither, I myself know not!

Wherefore, by the way, I would wish ye! employ not your little wits in certifying the world that I am gone to Rome, Jerusalem, Venice, or any other place at your idle appoint. I know, the best of ye, by the lies ye wrote of me, got not the price of a good hat to cover your brainless heads! If any of ye had come to me, my bounty should have exceeded the best of your good masters, the ballad buyers! I would have apparelled your dry pates in parti-coloured bonnets! and bestowed a leash of my cast[-off] bells to have crowned ye, with coxcombs!

I have made a privy search, what private Jigmonger of your jolly number hath been the Author of these abominable Ballets written of me.

I was told, it was the great Ballad-maker, T. D., alias *Thomas Deloney*, Chronicler of the memorable *Lives of the Six yeomen of the West, Jack of Newbury, the Gentle Craft*, &c., and such like honest men, omitted by Stow, Hollinshed, Grafton, Halle, Froissart, and all the rest of those well-deserving writers.

But I was given since to understand, your late General, Thomas, died poorly (as ye all must do!), and was honestly buried, which is much to be doubted of some of you!

The Quest of Inquiry [*inquest*] finding him, by death acquitted of the Indictment; I was let to wit, that another Lord of Little Wit, one whose employment for the Pageant was utterly spent, he being known to be Elderton's immediate heir,[2] was vehemently suspected: but, after due inquisition was made, he was at that time known to live like a man in a mist, having quite given over the mystery.

Still the Search continuing, I met a proper upright youth, only for a little stooping in the shoulder, all heart to the heel, a penny Poet; whose first making was the miserable stolen story of *Macdoel*, or *Macdobeth*, or *Mac*-somewhat:[3] for I am sure a *Mac* it was, though I never had the maw to see it: and he told me there was a fat filthy Ballet-maker that should have once been his journeyman to the trade, who lived about the town; and, ten to one! but he had thus terribly abused me and my Tabourer, for that he was able to do such a thing in print. A shrewd presumption!

I found him about the Bankside, sitting at a play. I desired to speak with him, had him to a tavern, charged [his] pipe with tobacco, and then laid this terrible accusation to his charge. He swells presently like one of the four winds. The violence of his breath blew the tobacco out of the pipe, and the heat of his wrath drank dry two bowls of Rhenish wine.

At length having power to speak, "Name my accuser!" saith he, "or I defie thee, KEMP! at the quart[er] staff!"

I told him! and all his anger turned to laughter; swearing "it did him good to have ill words of a hoddy doddy! a hobble de hoy!, a chicken! a squib! a squall! One that bath not wit enough to make a ballet; that by Pol and Aedipol would Pol his father, Derick his dad! do anything, how ill soever, to please his apish humour!"

I hardly believed this youth, that I took to be gracious, had been so graceless; but I heard, afterwards, his mother-in-law was eye-and ear-witness of his father's abuse, by this blessed child, on a public Stage, in "a merry Host of an Inn's" part.

Yet all this while, could not I find out the true ballet maker; till, by chance, a friend of mine pulled out of his pocket, a book in Latin, called *Mundus furiosus*, printed at Cullen [*Cologne*], written by one of the vilest and arrantest lying cullians [*wretches*] that ever wrote book; his name Jansonus: who, taking upon him to write an abstract of all the turbulent actions that had been lately attempted or performed in Christendom, like an unchristian wretch! writes only by report, partially, and scoffingly of such whose page's shoes he was unworthy to wipe. For indeed he is now dead. Farewell, he! every dog must have a day!

But see the luck on it! This beggarly lying busybody's

name brought out the Ballad-maker! and it was generally confirmed it was his kinsman! He confesses himself guilty, let any man look on his face! if there be not so red a colour that all the soap in the town will not wash white, let me be turned into a whiting, as I pass between Dover and Calais!

Well, God forgive thee, honest fellow!

I see, thou hast grace in thee! I prithee, do so no more! Leave writing these beastly ballets! make not good wenches, Prophetesses for little or no profit! nor for a sixpenny matter, revive not a poor fellow's fault that is hanged for his offence! it may be thine own destiny, one day: prithee, be good to them!

Call up, thy old Melpomene! whose strawberry quill may write the bloody lines of *the blue Lady*, and the *Prince of the burning crown*: a better subject I can tell ye! than your *Knight of the Red Cross*. So farewell! and cross me no more, I prithee! with thy rabble of bald rhymes, least at my return, I set a cross on thy forehead, that all men may know thee for a fool!

William Kemp

FINIS

---

1. Thomas Deloney was a silk weaver who became well known for his ballads as well as early fiction such as *Jack of Newbury* and *The Gentle Craft*.
2. William Elderton and his 'heir', Anthony Munday, were popular ballad writers of the day. Munday may have collaborated with Shakespeare.
3. This appears to suggest a ballad or play about Macbeth a few years before Shakespeare's c.1603–6 play.

www.ingramcontent.com/pod-product-compliance
Lightning Source LLC
Chambersburg PA
CBHW061501210726
48287CB00007B/2613
9781905315840